K

Christ Our Life

God Loves Us

AUTHORS

Sisters of Notre Dame of Chardon, Ohio

Sister Mary Kathleen Glavich, S.N.D.

Sister Jeanne Mary Nieminen, S.N.D.

CONSULTANTS

Marilyn Jones

Elaine Reardon

THEOLOGICAL ADVISOR

Sister Agnes Cunningham, S.S.C.M.

GENERAL EDITOR

Sister Mary Kathleen Glavich, S.N.D.

LOYOLAPRESS.

CHICAGO

Nihil Obstat: The Reverend Monsignor Joseph T. Moriarty, M.A., Censor Deputatus
Imprimatur: The Most Reverend Anthony M. Pilla, D.D., M.A., Bishop of Cleveland
Given at Cleveland, Ohio, on 5 March 1996

The *Nihil Obstat* and *Imprimatur* are official declarations that a book or pamphlet is free of doctrinal or moral error. No implication is contained therein that those who have granted the *Nihil Obstat* and *Imprimatur* agree with the contents, opinions, or statements expressed.

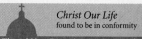

Christ Our Life
found to be in conformity

The Ad Hoc Committee to Oversee the Use of the Catechism, National Conference of Catholic Bishops, has found this catechetical series, copyright 1997 and 2002, to be in conformity with the *Catechism of the Catholic Church.*

ISBN: 0-8294-1544-0

Dedicated to St. Julie Billiart, foundress of the Sisters of Notre Dame, in gratitude for her inspiration and example

Acknowledgments

This present revision of the Christ Our Life series is the work of countless people. In particular, we acknowledge and thank the following for their roles in the project:

- The Sisters of Notre Dame who supported the production of the Christ Our Life series, especially Sister Mary Joell Overman, S.N.D.; Sister Mary Frances Murray, S.N.D.; and Sister Mary Margaret Hess, S.N.D.
- The Sisters of Notre Dame and others who over the past twenty years have shaped, written, and edited editions of the Christ Our Life series, in particular Sister Mary de Angelis Bothwell, S.N.D., the former editor, as well as those who worked on the previous edition of this kindergarten book: Sister Mary Verne Kavula, S.N.D.; Sister Mary Christa Jacobs, S.N.D.; Sister Carol Marie Urmetz, S.N.D.; Sister Mary Alicemarie Resley, S.N.D.; Sister Mary Loretta Tobin, S.N.D.; and Sister Mary Victoire Renk, S.N.D.
- Those who worked on different stages involved in producing this edition, especially Sister Mary Julie Boehnlein, S.N.D.; Sister Linda Marie Gecewicz, S.N.D.; Sister Mary Beth Gray, S.N.D.; Sister Joanmarie Harks, S.N.D.; Sister Rita Mary Harwood, S.N.D.; Sister Mary Nanette Herman, S.N.D.; Sister Mary Andrew Miller, S.N.D.; Sister Mary Catherine Rennecker, S.N.D.; and Sister Mary St. Jude Weisensell, S.N.D.
- Those catechists, directors of religious education, priests, parents, students, and others who responded to surveys, returned evaluation forms, wrote letters, or participated in interviews to help improve the series
- The personnel at Loyola Press who helped make our vision a reality

Scripture selections are taken from *The New American Bible,* copyright © 1991, 1986, 1970 by the Confraternity of Christian Doctrine, Washington, D.C., and are used by license of copyright owner. All rights reserved.

Excerpt from *The Jerusalem Bible,* copyright © 1966 by Darton, Longman & Todd, Ltd. and Doubleday, a division of Random House, Inc. Reprinted by Permission.

Excerpts from the English translation of *A Book of Prayers* © 1982, International Committee on English in the Liturgy, Inc. (ICEL); excerpts from the English translation of *Book of Blessings* © 1988, ICEL. All rights reserved.

All attempts possible have been made to contact the publisher for cited works in this book.

Photographs

© **Cleo Freelance Photography** (pp. 13, 18); © **Corbis Corp.** (p. 100 top); © **Digital Stock Corp.** (pp. 33, 83, 101 top, 103); © **EyeWire** (pp. 89, 91, 102 top); © **Myrleen Ferguson/PhotoEdit** (p. 72 bottom); © **Will Hart/PhotoEdit** (p. 9); © **Hillstrom Stock Photo, Inc.** (p. 99); © **Brent Jones** (p. 54A); © **Michael Newman/PhotoEdit** (p. 49); © **PhotoDisc, Inc.** (pp. 5, 14, 21, 29, 37, 41, 55, 75, 79, 87, 96, 101 bottom, 102 middle left and middle right and bottom, 107); © **Eugene D. Plaisted, O.S.C./Crosiers** (pp. i, iii, 84); © **Stacia Timonere** (pp. 68, 120); © **W. P. Wittman Limited** (pp. 17, 23, 25, 45, 59, 63, 67, 71, 72 top and middle, 73, 77, 100 bottom); © **Bruce Wodder/The Image Bank** (p. 95).

Artwork

Cheryl Arnemann (pp. 6–7, 8, 11, 12 bottom, 16 bottom, 19, 22, 24, 26–27, 30–31, 32, 36, 38, 39, 40, 44, 48 bottom, 51, 52, 54D top left and right, 56–57, 58, 69, 88–89, 92–93, 94, 97, 110); **Len Ebert/PC&F Inc.** (p. 54D bottom right); **Diana Magnuson** (pp. 64–65, 76, 86); **Mike Muir** (pp. 15, 20, 34–35, 36, 42, 43, 46, 47, 50, 53 bottom, 54, 54D bottom left, 60–61, 62, 70, 85, 104–105, 106, 108 bottom, 109, 111, 112, 113, 114, 115, 117 bottom, 118–119, 120, punchouts); **Eileen Mueller Neill & Kelly Neill** (pp. 54B, 106A, 106C); **Proof Positive/Farrowlyne Assoc., Inc.** (pp. 10 bottom, 12 top, 48 top, 54C, 106B, 108 top); **Dan Siculan** (pp. 66, 74 bottom, 78 bottom, 80, 81 bottom, 82 bottom, 90 bottom, 98 bottom); **Robert Voigts** (pp. 10 top, 23, 53 top, 74 top, 78 top, 81 top, 82 top, 90 top, 98 top, 102, 116, 117 top).

Cover design by Donald Kye.
Cover art © Eugene D. Plaisted, O.S.C./Crosiers.

00 01 02 03 04 05 06 6 5 4 3 2 1

LoyolaPress.

3441 N. Ashland Avenue
Chicago, Illinois 60657
(800) 621-1008

CONTENTS

K

Notes to Parents

As parents, you have a sacred trust! You are the primary religious educators of your child. God calls you to nurture not only the natural life of your child but also your child's grace life received at baptism. This responsibility requires that you grow in faith yourselves and that you share your faith with your family. Here are some steps to deepen your relationship with God and with your family this year:

- Set aside a time (about 15 minutes) and a quiet place for private prayer each day. Read the Bible, Bible commentaries, or spiritual books and listen to the Lord speak to you. Respond to him.

- Set aside a time for family prayer each day.

- Celebrate the Eucharist on Sundays or Saturday evenings as a family, if possible. Children learn much from your example of prayer.

- Make reconciliation, forgiving and being forgiven, a part of family living. Celebrate the Sacrament of Reconciliation (Penance) regularly.

- Attend programs scheduled for adult education in your parish.

- Involve your whole family in service projects for the Church and civic community.

In addition to experiencing God's love in your family, your child will learn more about his love through the religious education program.

The first semester kindergarten program, *God Loves Us,* is designed to make the children aware of God's love through the many good and beautiful persons, events, and things he has placed in their lives. Each chapter leads the children to appreciate their uniqueness and to sense God's presence in all the wonderful things around them.

The second semester kindergarten program, *We Love God,* continues the themes of the first semester. It also leads the children to a greater desire to love God in return through their prayers and acts of kindness for others.

The family section of your child's book, usually located on the first page of each chapter, briefs you on the religious concept developed with the children in class and offers suggestions for living the message in your family. Since the children's text contains the message, you are encouraged to read it over with your child each week. However, it is advisable not to read chapters to your child until after they have been presented in class. After you read the family notes and use some of the follow-up activities, please write your name or initials on the line provided. Each unit ends with Family Feature pages that suggest family customs and provide review activities.

May God continue to bless you and your family and, in the words of St. Paul, "may he give you the power through his Spirit for your hidden self to grow strong, so that Christ may live in your hearts through faith" (Ephesians 3:16 JB).

Welcomes Are Good

To be near God is . . . good.

Psalm 73:28

WELCOMES IN FAMILIES

The Message

When we open ourselves to others, we become better able to welcome the Lord into our lives. In this chapter, the children are encouraged to reach out to others and make them feel welcome. They learn that Jesus loves and welcomes children, and that he wants them to know him.

Activities

- Read pages 5–8 with your child and let him/her tell you about them.
- Train your child to greet visitors politely and to offer simple gestures of hospitality, such as inviting them to be seated.
- Use Psalm 73:28 as part of your family prayers this week.

❑ Signature

Welcomes are like warm sunshine.

Jesus welcomed little children.

He said, "Let the children come to me."

Mark 10:14

Jesus loves children.

Jesus welcomes us.

He wants us to know him.

Jesus loves us.

Others welcome us.

We welcome others.

- Put an X under the persons you might welcome today.
- Touch the pictures and think how you will greet each person.

O Lord, how great is your name, over all the earth.

Based on Psalm 8:2

NAMES IN FAMILIES

The Message

To pronounce the name of Jesus reverently is to show respect for his person. In this chapter the children talk about the importance of names. They are led to experience the mystery and transcendence of God by becoming aware that Jesus' name is holy.

Activities

• Ask your child to tell about pages 9–12 as you read them.

• Share with your child the significance of his or her name—its meaning and why it was chosen. Encourage your child to greet by name the people he or she meets. Put the Jesus name card in a place where it will remind your family to call upon the name of Jesus in times of need and thanksgiving.

• Use Psalm 8:2 as part of your family prayers this week.

_____

❏ Signature

Kristin   Mary

Miquel   Larry

Angelo   Henry

LArry

My name is ___Brat_____.

When someone calls us by name, we feel good.

Jesus is God.

His name is holy.

We say Jesus' name with love.

God tells us his name.
He l♥ves us.

Jesus' name is holy.

JESUS

 Do

❖ Color the letters in Jesus' name with pretty colors.

❖ Show that the name is holy. Draw yellow lines shining out from all around it.

❖ Look at Jesus' name and say it with love.

Books are full of stories.
Stories can make us laugh or cry,
open wide our eyes with wonder,
or even squeal with joy.

THE BIBLE IN FAMILIES

The Message

God reveals himself to us whenever Sacred Scripture is read. When we listen or read with faith, we are led to understand God's action working in our lives—calling us to commit ourselves to him. The children learn that the Bible, which has Jesus' story in it, is a holy book that tells about God's love for us. They learn that God's people listen to readings from the Bible at Mass.

Activities

• Encourage your child to tell you about pages 13–16. Let him or her talk about the class activities, which included having the children tell about themselves.

• Enthrone a Bible by placing it reverently on a table. Have your child tell about God's message of love to us in the Bible.

• Begin reading short, appropriate sections of the Bible (or a child's Bible) to your child. You might choose Mark 10:13–16, Jeremiah 31:3, and parts of Genesis 1.

• Use Psalm 78:4 as a prayer before reading from the Bible.

• Encourage your child to listen quietly to the Liturgy of the Word at Mass.

❏ Signature _____

The Bible is a holy book.
It tells the story of God's love for us.

The Bible tells the wonderful story of Jesus.
He came to show us God's love.

God's people listen to his story.

We will tell the wonderful things the LORD has done.

Based on Psalm 78:4

A Story from God's Book

1. Jonah runs away.

2. A storm comes.

3. A whale swallows Jonah.

4. Jonah lands where God wants him.

5. He preaches and people listen.

6. God loves all people.

 Do

✜ Tell the story of Jonah.
✜ Think how much God loves us.

This is what the stories in the Bible tell us.

God

Loves

Us

 Do

✤ Color the heart red or pink.
✤ Read what the Bible tells us.
✤ What would you like to tell God?

God's World Is Good

4

Blue skies
Spotted giraffes
Hoppity rabbits
Puddles to splash.

Green grass
Tickle my toes
People with hugs
A baby that grows.

Red-ripe apples
Trees to climb
Sandy beaches
Shells to find.

God made this
wonderful
world!

CREATION AND FAMILIES

The Message
The entire cosmos is a representation of God and makes him present to us. In this chapter the children are led to see how the wonderful works of creation speak to us of God's goodness and love.

Activities
- Read over pages 17–20 with your child and let him or her tell you about them and the class activities.

- Go on a family walk—perhaps in a park—to enjoy nature. Let each person name a gift of God he or she sees.
- Use Psalm 33:5 as part of your family prayers this week. Invite your child to lead you in praying it.
- Read aloud Genesis 1:31 and appropriate sections from Psalms 65, 66, and 104.

❑ Signature

God made the world for us.
The Bible tells us so.
All the good things in the world
    tell us about God.
They tell us that God loves us.

The earth is full of the goodness of the LORD.

Based on Psalm 33:5

God's world is full of
wonderful things like

twinkly stars,

beautiful flowers,

and furry kittens.

 Do

✢ Make the stars twinkle.
✢ Make pretty flowers grow on the plants.
✢ Make the little kittens furry.

In the Bible God made Noah a promise.
God promised to love everything on earth always.
The rainbow is a sign of God's love.

 Do

✤ Circle the animals you find in the clouds.

✤ Smile to show God you are happy with the beautiful things he made.

✤ Say thank you to God.

My heart is quiet within me, O LORD.

Based on Psalm 131:2

QUIET IN FAMILIES

The Message

Silence helps us enter into our innermost selves and encounter God present within us. In this chapter the children learn that good and beautiful things happen in quiet. Through a guided reflection, they commune with God present within them.

Activities

• Encourage your child to tell about the class prayer experiences as you read over pages 21–24.

• Learn to be comfortable with quiet by periodically refraining from turning on the radio, stereo, or TV.

• Schedule a family quiet hour for personal prayer, reflection, or reading. Family members may take turns reading the Bible and other books to younger children, who should listen silently.

• Help your child practice self-control as preparation for prayer. Encourage him or her to keep clothes and other belongings in order and to speak quietly and politely.

❑ Signature

SH- SH- SH

Quiet is

clouds moving across the sky

my
mother's
touch

yellow
butterflies

dancing
in the sun

green grass growing in the yard

a warm and happy feeling deep inside

SH-SH-SH

Quiet helps us enter into our hearts.
We meet God there.

Jesus says, "I am with you always."
He is with us in a special way in church.

God loves us.

Quiet helps us to think of God.

It helps us to love God.

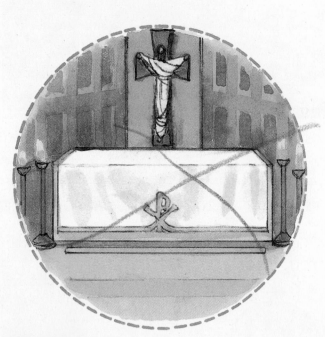

 Do

❖ Draw bubbles around the pictures that show quiet times that help you think of God.

❖ Think of God and love God as you work.

Fill us in the morning with your love.
Based on Psalm 90:14

PRAYER IN FAMILIES

The Message

Through prayer we encounter God and converse familiarly with him. Prayer will become a part of your child's life if it is an evident part of yours. In this chapter the children learn that prayer can include reflection, speech, gestures, music, song, and dance. They participate in a variety of prayer experiences.

Activities

- As you read over pages 25–28 with your child, encourage him or her to tell you about the different ways the class prayed to God.

- Let your child see you at prayer and hear you call upon God in times of joy and sorrow.
- Decide on a regular time for daily family prayer.
- Obtain a prayer candle to be lit at family prayer. Place it near the enthroned Bible, so your family has a worship center around which to gather for prayer.
- Read Romans 5:5 to your family.
- Help your child respond to the beauty and goodness in our world and see them as reflections of God.

❏ Signature

We like to talk to those we love:
"Mom, I like your new suit."
"Please may I wear my blue jacket today?"
"Look at those beautiful flowers."

"Dad, I love you so very much."
"Thank you for letting me play."
"I'm sorry I didn't do what I should."
"I'll try to be good today."

We can talk to God.

We can say,

"I love you."

"Thank you, God."

"I'm sorry, God."

"Please help me be good today."

God always listens.

God

us.

When we talk to God, we pray.

God bless

Do

- Finish the prayer by putting a circle around the people you want to pray for.
- Remember you can talk to God any time you want.
- You can pray to God in different ways.

LORD, from my birth I was in your care.

Based on Psalm 22:11

GOD'S LOVE IN FAMILIES

The Message

Jesus reveals that God is the Father of us all and that we are to be as brothers and sisters in his family. The children talk about families and learn that all members contribute to making a happy family. They learn that they belong to the human family, to God's family, the Church, and call God "Father." They are introduced to the first two lines of the Our Father prayer. Place the Our Father prayer card your child brought home in a special place of honor.

Activities

• Let your child tell you about pages 29–32.

• If children are to grow physically, psychologically, and spiritually, they need to know they are loved. Give your child and other family members special signs of affection this week. Show your child pictures of his or her baptism.

• Proclaim a Family Week. Select a different member to honor at the family meal each day. Take turns telling the honored member one thing you especially like about him or her.

• Pray the Our Father together each day as a family. You might pray it at the family meal with joined hands.

❑ Signature

29

Kittens belong to their cat family.

Bunnies belong to their rabbit family.

Ducks belong to their duck family.

God made us to belong to families, too.

Families are the people we live with.

Jesus lived with Mary and Joseph.
They were the Holy Family.

We belong to the family of people all over the world.

We are all brothers and sisters.

We belong to God's special family, the Church.

We joined the Church when we were baptized.

God is our Father. We pray,

"Our Father, who art in heaven, hallowed be thy name."

Our heavenly Father watches over us with gentle care.

He l♥ves us.

We belong to God's family.
We are his children.
He is our Father.

Do

- Draw lines to show to which family each one belongs.
- Thank God for your family.

I Am Good

I thank you, O LORD, for the wonder of myself.

Based on Psalm 139:14

SELF-CONCEPT IN FAMILIES

The Message

We are made in God's image and are called to share eternal life with him. In this chapter the children learn that God made them and considers them very precious. They engage in activities designed to help them appreciate themselves as worthwhile persons.

Activities

• Read over pages 33–36.
• Encourage the members of your family to note and praise one another's successes.

• Refrain from helping your child before it is needed. This shows you have trust in your child's abilities.
• Let family members make their own decisions whenever possible.
• Show respect and appreciation for the work of each family member.

_____

❑ Signature

Henry

Hey, wake me! Wake me!
Time to walk
Listening for the flowers' talk!
See me! See me!
Wrinkling my nose,
Smelling a rose.
Me! Me! Wrinkle-nose, wonderful me!

Swing me! Push me!
Way up high.
I need to get me a piece of sky.

Hey, watch me! Watch me!
Go down the slide,
Taking a ride.
Fly me! Fly me!
Round and round
'Til I flop dizzy to the ground.
Me! Me! Dizzyhead, wonderful me!

Catch me! Catch me!
Here I come
Zooming right into your open arms.

Feed me! Feed me!
I'm weak in the knees.
Some peanut butter and jelly, please.
Hold me! Hold me!
Squeeze me tight.
Now's the time to kiss good night.
Me! Me! Sleepyhead, wonderful me!

God made me.

I can do all kinds of wonderful things.

I thank God for making wonderful ME.

God made me wonderful.

God l♥ves me.

I am good. God made me wonderful.

I can hear	
I can taste	
I can touch	
I can smell	
I can see	

 Do

✢ Make an X on each picture that does not go with the words above.

✢ Draw something you like to look at.

✢ Did you thank God for making you so wonderful?

Growing Is Good

I am like a green olive tree growing before the LORD.

Based on Psalm 52:10

GROWING IN FAMILIES

The Message

Our growth is a lifelong process consisting of never-ending struggles and new challenges. Baptism is the beginning of a new way of life, and with the help of the Holy Spirit we can grow into the likeness of Christ. Choosing baptism for your child indicated your willingness to foster his or her Christian growth. In this chapter the children learn that at baptism they become members of the Church.

Activities

• Read over pages 37–40 with your child.

• Show your child's baby book to him or her and tell some "growing-up" stories.
• Look at old family pictures so that your child learns that everyone grows and changes.
• Show your child his or her baptismal certificate and robe.
• Tell your child why you decided to have him or her baptized.
• Celebrate everyone's anniversary of baptism.
• Talk about ways your child can be more loving.

❑ Signature

Pumpkins grow.

Birds grow.

Elephants grow.

We grow.

We grow bigger

and bigger

and bigger.

We keep growing in some way all of our lives.

We were baptized.

We became Christians.

We became members of God's family.

We grow in Jesus' love.

We grow more like Jesus.

God, our Father, l❤ves us.

 Do

✣ Make the olive tree grow. Put more branches, leaves, and flowers on it.

✣ Tell God you want to grow more like Jesus.

✣ Put perfume on your tree. It will remind you of Jesus' love.

✣ Tell Jesus you will spread his love everywhere.

Thanking Is Good

We give you thanks, LORD, for you are good.

Based on Psalm 136:1

THANKSGIVING IN FAMILIES

The Message

In giving thanks to God, we acknowledge that all things have been created by him, belong to him, and come to us through his goodness. Thanksgiving provides an occasion for families to reflect and express gratitude. Mealtime is a daily opportunity to pray together. In this chapter the children hear about special times when we thank God. They discover that "thank yous" are for every day. They begin to memorize the traditional grace before meals and color a prayer card for the table at home as a reminder to pray grace. In a prayer celebration they thank God for their blessings.

Activities

- Read over pages 41–44 with your child and let him/her tell you about them.

- Proclaim a "family thank-you meal." Take turns thanking each person for his or her special contribution to the family.
- Place the grace prayer card by a different person each day, indicating whose turn it is to lead meal prayers.
- On Thanksgiving, participate in the Eucharist and take an offering of food or money for the poor.
- At grace time, let each person thank God for a blessing received during the year.
- Have a family renewal in the use of the magic words "please" and "thank you."

❏ Signature

The words "Thank you" are
magic and cast a magic spell.

They tell the way we feel as no
other words can tell.

Saying thank you makes us happy
to see what joy we brought.

The magic words "Thank you"
are words we use a lot.

Father, We Thank You

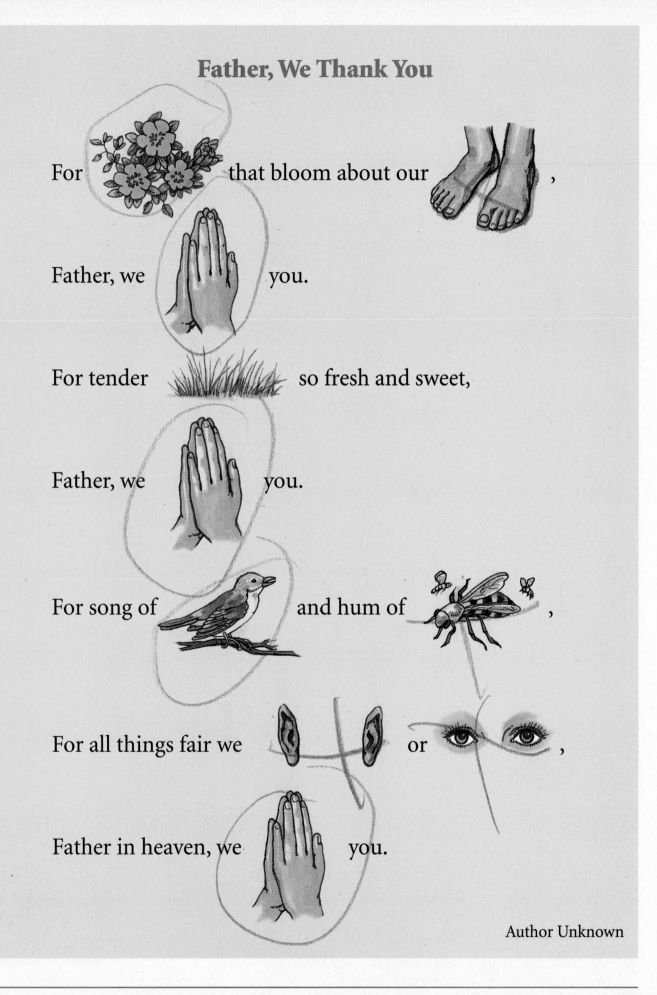

For [flowers] that bloom about our [feet],

Father, we [thank] you.

For tender [grass] so fresh and sweet,

Father, we [thank] you.

For song of [bird] and hum of [bee],

For all things fair we [hear] or [see],

Father in heaven, we [thank] you.

Author Unknown

We thank God for many gifts.

Thank you, God, for . . .

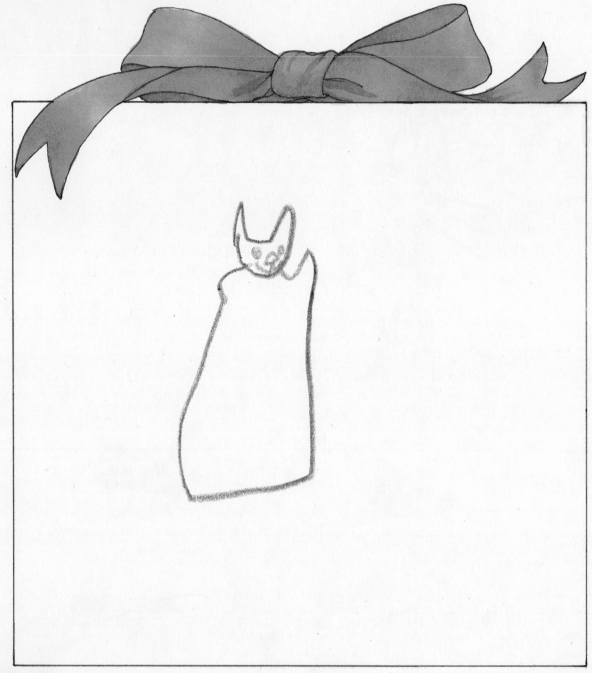

Do

* Think of the gifts for which you wish to
  thank God.
* Draw pictures of some of them in the box.
* Touch each gift and thank God for it.

Oh Lᴏʀᴅ, I wait for you all day long.

Based on Psalm 25:5

ADVENT IN FAMILIES

The Message

Advent is the season of waiting and preparing to celebrate the threefold coming of Christ: his coming long ago as a man, his daily comings in grace through the sacraments and the events of our daily lives, and his future coming in glory. The children learn that Christmas commemorates the birthday of God's Son, Jesus, who came to help us be good. They make an Advent wreath and understand it as a sign of preparing for Jesus. Place it on your table as a reminder. Add "Come, Lord Jesus!" to your meal prayers.

Activities

- Set up a stable without the figures of Jesus, Mary, and Joseph. Put the animals in the empty stable. Place the shepherds and sheep a short distance away.
- Place a small box of hay (yellow paper cut in fine strips) in front of the stable. Each day put a piece of straw in the stable for every kind act performed.
- On Christmas Eve, let everyone help to place the figures of Jesus, Mary, and Joseph in the stable. Sing "Silent Night."

❑ Signature

Christmas is coming.

We get ready.

We decorate Christmas trees.

Decorate this tree.

We wrap gifts.

Color the ribbon on the gift.

We help make cookies and
good things to eat.

Make a red cherry on
each Christmas cookie.

Christmas is Jesus' birthday.

God, our Father, sent Jesus to us on the first Christmas.

Jesus came to help us be good.

Jesus' birthday is coming.

We prepare our hearts as gifts.

We will be loving to others.

We give Jesus the gift of our love.

Do

- Think how you will bring Jesus' love to someone.
- Draw a picture of it in the heart.
- Pray, "Come, Lord Jesus."

God shows me the way to choose.

Based on Psalm 25:12

CHOOSING IN FAMILIES

The Message

Mary, the perfect follower of Jesus, shows us that we attain happiness and self-fulfillment by loving surrender in obedience to God's will. By their choices, family members contribute to family unity or take away from it. The self-control and good habits your child learns now lay the foundation for a moral life. In this chapter the children learn the importance of making good choices. They learn that Mary is their mother and will help them do what God wants.

Activities

- Assist your child with the Hail Mary prayer printed on the back of the Mary card he or she brings home.

- Point out the happiness your child's good actions bring to the family and the pain bad actions cause.
- Let your child make decisions and encourage him or her to stand by them.
- Refuse to let your child blame others for his or her failings. Guide him or her to admit being at fault.
- Let your child know what is acceptable behavior at home and in public and expect conformity. Give reasons for what you ask your child to do.
- Let your child know he or she is loved even when naughty and disagreeable.

❑ Signature

We should think before we choose.

We want to choose what is good.

What is good will make us happy.

CHOOSE:

✤   a good snack

✤   a good pet
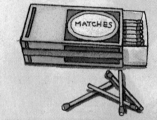 

✤   something good
to play with

✤   a good place to play

 Do

✤   Circle each one that is good to choose.

God our Father chose a mother for his Son.

He chose Mary.

Mary loved God.

She would be a good mother for Jesus.

Mary chose to do what God wanted.

She said yes to God.

YES

Mary helps us say yes.

God loves Mary and us.

Do

❖ Make pretty flowers around Mary's YES.

❖ Color her dress carefully to make it look beautiful.

❖ Touch the YES and say yes to God with Mary.

God is good.

God gives us many gifts
and wants us to be happy.

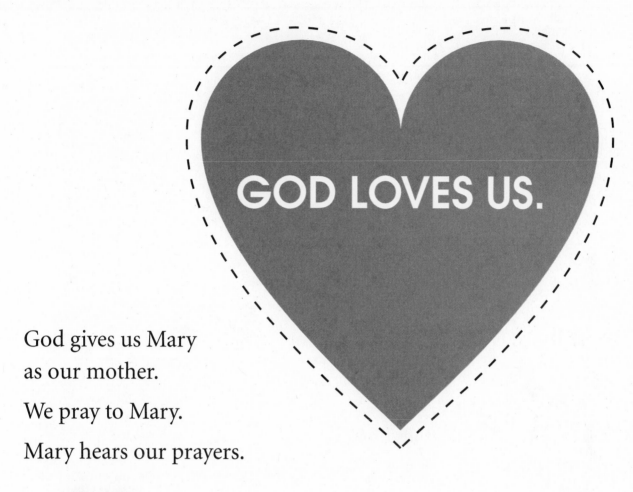

GOD LOVES US.

God gives us Mary
as our mother.

We pray to Mary.

Mary hears our prayers.

We love God and Mary.

Do

✤ Trace around the heart with a red crayon.
✤ Draw yourself. Show how happy you are when
you do what God wants.
✤ Ask Mary to help you say yes to God.

Prayer to Mary

Hail , full of grace.

The Lord is with .

Blessed are you among .

And blessed is the fruit of your womb, .

Holy , Mother of God,

 for us sinners

now and at the  of our death. Amen.

❖ Color the frame around the prayer.

Giving Family Blessings

Mr. and Mrs. Matias and their three children are from the Philippines. The family shows affection not only by kisses and hugs. Sometimes the children take the hand of their mother or father and press it to their forehead. While this practice is not common among American families, family blessings are a beautiful custom. You will find that it binds you more closely together and centers you in God.

The *Catechism of the Catholic Church* points out that "every baptized person is called to be a 'blessing' and to bless" (1669). Parents have every right to bless their children and call down God's goodness on them. The blessing may be done by tracing a cross on the forehead of the child or by putting a hand or hands on or over the child's head. Words may be a simple "God bless you" or a personal prayer such as "May God be with you and keep you safe tonight." The blessing may be done with holy water, which recalls the child's baptism when he or she became a child of God.

Blessings might be bestowed at the following times:

- before the children go to bed
- before the children leave the home
- on a special occasion
- for a birthday
- for a baptismal anniversary
- for a name day
- in time of trouble
- during sickness

The book *Catholic Household Blessings and Prayers* contains Scripture readings and prayers for various family blessings. This book and smaller books of blessings are published by the United States Catholic Conference in Washington and may be ordered by calling 1-800-235-8722.

Being a Blessing

Encourage your child to be a blessing to the family. Each time your child chooses to help or obeys cheerfully, he or she may add a flower to the blessing basket. Keep this picture posted on the refrigerator or family bulletin board.

Thanks for Life

Discuss things your child can do, such as skip, sing, or see a sunset. Have him or her draw one thing and make up a prayer of thanks about it. Print the prayer below the picture.

Talking to Friends

Help your child pray to the people shown here:

Jesus

Mary

Joseph

Guardian Angel

The LORD is my shepherd; I shall not want.

Based on Psalm 23:1

SHEPHERDING IN FAMILIES

The Message

The relationship of love and trust that should exist between the human person and Christ is exemplified in the parable of the Good Shepherd. We are all called to be shepherds in some way. Parents must answer for their children's religious formation, and catechists for the message they give the children. Children must be responsible for their pets and are sometimes made responsible for younger brothers and sisters. In this chapter the children learn of the protective love Jesus has for each of them as they hear the parable of the Good Shepherd. They receive a Good Shepherd cutout set that they may set up at home as a reminder of Jesus' constant concern for them.

Activities

- Invite your child to say or sing Psalm 23:1. Have your child use the Good Shepherd cutouts to tell the parable.
- Say or do something to let your child experience your loving care.
- Give your child a pet (such as a goldfish) or a plant to care for. Caring for someone or something is a beautiful way to grow in appreciation for the loving care bestowed on us. It also helps develop qualities of concern and responsibility.
- Let your child see your special care for young or elderly family members and let him or her assist in some small way.

❑ Signature

A shepherd loves
and cares for his sheep.

Jesus said, "The shepherd of
the sheep enters the
sheepfold through the gate.

He calls the sheep by name.

When the shepherd brings
the sheep out,
he walks ahead to lead them.

The sheep follow because
they know his voice."
Based on John 10:1–5

Jesus said, "I am the
good shepherd.

I know my sheep.
They know me.

I call them by name.

I am willing to die for my
sheep."
Based on John 10:14–16

Jesus loves and cares for us.

We ❤ love Jesus, the Good Shepherd.

 Do

✤ Trace the staff and color it brown. Color the wolf gray or brown.

✤ Jesus, the Good Shepherd, knows you and calls you by name. What do you want to tell him?

14 Hearts Are Good

LORD, your kindness reaches to heaven.

Based on Psalm 36:6

LOVING IN FAMILIES

The Message

God's love was fully revealed to us in Jesus. The Christian religion is based on a love relationship between God and the human person. Children must realize that they are personally loved by God. They need to accept themselves as persons worthy to be loved by God and others. In this chapter the children hear again of God's great love for them shown through Jesus and through the loving persons God places in their lives. They are invited to share in Jesus' love by showing love for others. They hear about Jesus' love for his friends in the story of the large catch of fish and cooking breakfast (John 21:1–14).

Activities

- Read over pages 59–62 with your child and let your child tell about them.
- Give a hug to each family member today to let each one know that he or she is loved.
- Make a point to say or do something each day to make every member feel loved and appreciated.
- Let your child tell about the heart pin received as a reminder of Jesus' love for others.
- Help your child to look upon loving and caring adults as bringing God's love to him or her.
- Praise your child's efforts to be loving. Point out the joy he or she brings to others by loving actions.

❏ Signature

Love is a special gift God put in our hearts.
It makes others happy.
God sent Jesus into the world to show us his love.

Jesus loves everyone.

Jesus wants us to love everyone, too.

He says, "Love one another as I love you."

Based on John 13:34

We l♥ve God, our Father.

Jesus showed love for his friends.

We bring Jesus' love to others.

 Do

✤ Connect the dots from 1 to 10 to make what Jesus gave his friends. Color it.

✤ Draw a fire on the sticks where Jesus cooked breakfast for his friends.

✤ Thank God for the gift of love.

Our helping hands are gifts of love.
With them, we give to others.
We show the love that's in our hearts
For our sisters and our brothers.

Our hands can bring us blessings, too,
For they help us share our love.
Their loving deeds bring happiness,
And special joys from God above.

Our hands can bring our gifts to God,
When we pray to him each day.
We join our hands in prayer and love
That we may follow in his way.

O God, your right hand has upheld me.

Based on Psalm 18:36

SERVICE IN FAMILIES

The Message

Jesus made it known through his words and actions that he came not to be served, but to serve. He taught the way of self-giving as the way to human fulfillment. Children find meaning in life through love of God and others if they live in families in which they witness generous self-giving service. In this chapter the children hear the story of Jesus helping two blind men by his healing touch. They learn that Jesus calls them to be helpers, too.

Activities

• Read over pages 63–66 with your child.
• Praise your child for helping others and for work well done.
• Let your child see your willingness to help those both inside and outside your family circle.
• Adopt an elderly person in your neighborhood. Have your child make a card or gift for the person.
• Assign a small chore for which your child is responsible each day.

❏ Signature

Two blind men heard that Jesus was passing by.

They shouted, "Lord, have mercy on us!"

Jesus stopped and asked, "What do you want me to do for you?"

They said, "Lord, let us see."

Jesus felt sorry for them.

He touched their eyes.

They could see.

The two men followed Jesus, praising God.

Based on Matthew 20:30–34

Jesus helped people.

We will help people, too.

We will show

our

love

for God.

I can use my hands to help others.

Do

❖ Draw a line under the pictures that show how YOU can help.

❖ How does it make you feel when you have helped?

❖ Thank God for the gift of your helping hands.

Being Sorry Is Good

I am sorry for doing wrong.

Based on Psalm 32:5

FEELINGS IN FAMILIES

The Message

Although feelings enrich our lives, in themselves they are neither good nor bad. We all have a need to admit our feelings and to take responsibility for the way we express them. Children who live in families where forgiving and being forgiven are part of life easily learn to accept God's forgiveness. In this chapter the children explore some of their feelings and are made aware of others' feelings. They learn that it is wrong to hurt themselves, to hurt others, or to damage property when angry. They learn how to say "I'm sorry" when they hurt someone's feelings, and they hear Jesus tell them to forgive those who hurt them.

Activities

- Read over pages 67–70 with your child and let him or her tell you about them.
- Show sensitivity in your family toward one another's feelings. Do not encourage repressing feelings, but teach your child how to deal with them.
- Be careful not to make your child feel guilt where there is none.
- Readily say "I'm sorry" when you have shown impatience or anger.
- Help your child learn how to apologize. Show how to make amends by sharing a treat or making a gift or card for the one who has been hurt.

❑ Signature

It is not easy to always be loving.
It is not easy to always do what
pleases God.

Sometimes we hurt others on
purpose.

This is a sin.
When we sin, we are not happy.

But we can say, "I'm sorry."
Then we will be happy again.

Jesus wants us to be good children of God.

When we have not been good, we are like lost sheep.

We should tell Jesus we are sorry.

Jesus forgives those who are sorry.

We try to be God's loving children again.

Jesus said, "Forgive others from your heart."

Based on Matthew 18:35

We forgive like Jesus.

We forgive those who hurt us.

We show our love for God.

Jesus forgave Zacchaeus, a thief.

I'M SORRY

Do

- Find Zacchaeus in the tree. Circle him.
- Find three lost sheep in the field. Circle them.
- Trace over the letters.
- Think about whether there is someone you should say "I'm sorry" to.

70

I am glad when I go to God's house.

Based on Psalm 122:1

THE CHURCH IN FAMILIES

The Message

Catholic Christians first receive spiritual life at Baptism. This life is strengthened with Confirmation and nourished through the Eucharist. Throughout life, we grow in our realization of what incorporation into Jesus' passion, death, and resurrection really means. It is through their parents' faith that children first learn what it is to be Catholic Christians, witnessing to Jesus and his Church in today's world. In this chapter, the children hear again that they belong to the Church through Baptism. They learn of the role of the priest and of other members of the parish community.

- Take your child to visit your parish church and let him or her ask you about various things there. Share a treat afterward.
- Have your child go to Sunday Mass with you. Greet people as you enter. Let your child greet the priest and meet other parishioners after Mass.
- Use the Our Father as part of your family prayer. Join hands as you pray together.
- Encourage your child's participation in both the Our Father and Lord, Have Mercy at Mass.
- Talk with your child about the ways parishioners help the parish and participate in the Mass.

Activities

- Read over pages 71–74 with your child.

❏ Signature

The Church is a family of people who believe in Jesus.

These people want to follow Jesus' way of love.

They gather together to praise God and to remember Jesus.

God's family comes together in a special building.

This building is called a church because the people who gather there are the Church.

Jesus is present in the church building in a special way.

I belong to _____.
(Help children print the name of their church.)

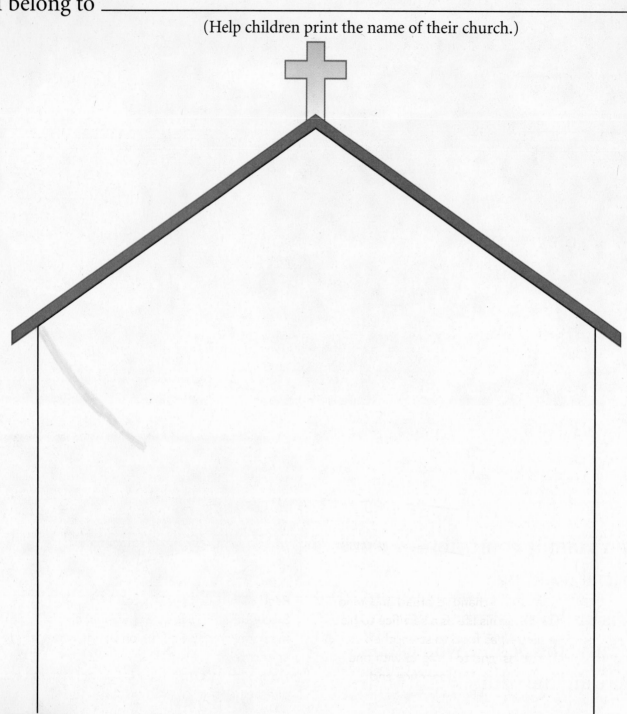

Do

♣ Draw a picture of something you have seen in God's house.

♣ Thank God that you belong to the Church.

♣ Tell God what you like about his house, the church building.

18

LORD, you give us bread to make us strong.

Based on Psalm 104:14–15

SHARING MEALS IN FAMILIES

The Message

At the Last Supper Jesus changed bread and wine into himself. He offered his life as a sacrifice to his Father. He gave himself as food to strengthen us, to unite himself with us, and to unite us with one another. The Mass, then, is both sacrifice and meal. In this chapter, the children learn that meals are times for sharing love as well as for sharing food. They hear the story of Jesus' Last Supper and learn that at Mass Jesus offers himself up for us and feeds us with the bread and wine that are his Body and Blood. Through love and friendship shared at family meals, children experience the human values found in the Eucharist.

Activities

- Read with your child pages 75–78.
- Discuss the day's activities as a family at mealtime, with emphasis on things important to your child.
- Have a family bread-baking project and enjoy the bread at your family meal.
- Let your child help make a cake or cookies or help plan a meal.
- Discuss how coming to meals on time shows love.
- Give your child the job of setting the table.
- Sit in church where your child can easily see what is happening during Mass.
- Be early enough for Sunday Mass to have time to settle down before Mass begins.

❑ Signature

Jesus ate with his apostles on the night before he died.
It was his last supper with them.

At this meal, Jesus gave thanks and praise to his Father.

He changed bread and wine into himself.
He offered himself to his Father for us.
He gave himself to his apostles as food and drink.
Then he said, "Do this in memory of me."

As God's family, we come together at Mass.
We give God thanks and praise.

We hear God's Word in the Bible.

We remember that Jesus died for all of us.

We see God's people receive the holy bread and holy wine
that are Jesus.
We belong to God's family, the Catholic Church.
We, too, will receive Jesus when we are older.

At Mass the bread and wine become Jesus.
God's people eat the holy bread.

Sometimes they drink
from the cup.

They receive Jesus
in Holy Communion.

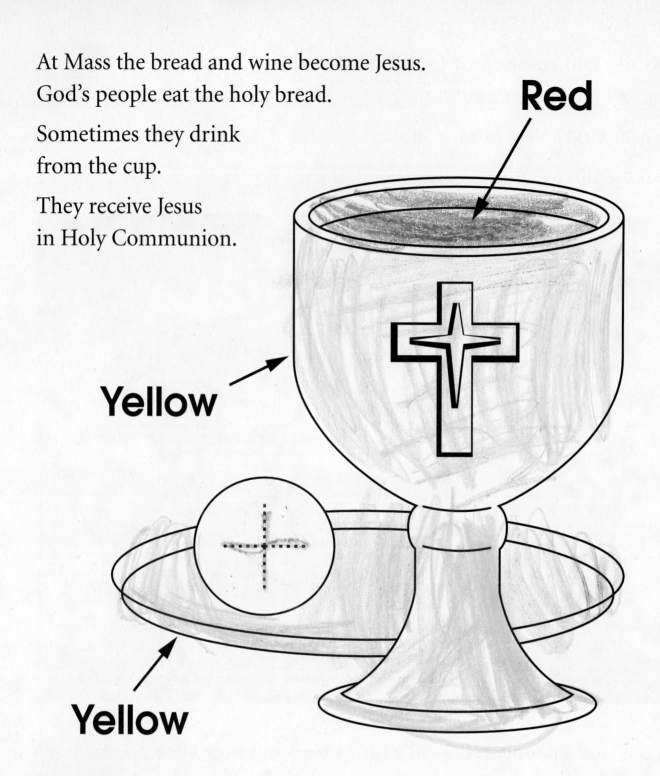

Red

Yellow

Yellow

Do

✢ Color the wine in the cup red.
✢ Color the cup and plate yellow.
✢ Trace over the cross on the bread.
✢ Where do you see bread and a cup like this?

Put a seed into the ground
To die so a plant can grow.
With sun and water from God,
New life sprouts and starts to show.

Apple seeds make apple trees,
Potato seeds, potatoes.
Radish seeds grow radishes,
Tomato seeds, tomatoes.

Flower seeds grow marigolds,
Violets, and roses, too.
Each seed that dies and grows
Tells God's love for me and you.

God sent his Son that we might live.

Based on John 3:17

THE CROSS IN FAMILIES

The Message

Christ's death and resurrection is the central mystery of our faith. Through the cross, Jesus freed us from slavery to sin and death, and became the source of our supernatural life. After the consecration at Mass, we proclaim in the Memorial Acclamation that "Christ has died, Christ is risen, Christ will come again." Then we live what we proclaim by accepting the cross in the dyings and risings that are part of our life. The children are introduced to the mystery of life and death through a seed that dies to give new life to a plant. They learn that through Jesus' cross, they received new life in baptism to enable them to live in love as Jesus did. Find a good place for the cross your child brought home to use when saying daily prayers.

Activities

- Read pages 79–82 with your child. Let your child plant some seeds in a pot or make a small garden. Talk about the way a seed dies to give life to a plant.
- Trace a cross on your child's forehead when you say your "good night."
- Teach your child to make the Sign of the Cross with the right hand: In the name of the Father (touch the forehead), and of the Son (touch the breast), and of the Holy (touch the left shoulder) Spirit (touch the right shoulder). Amen (fold hands). Your reverent making of this sign will impress your child.
- Encourage your child to make the Sign of the Cross with holy water when entering a church.

❑ Signature

A seed dies to give a plant new life.
Jesus died to give us new life
so we can live in love as Jesus did.

✤ Glue a seed in the hole.
✤ Draw the new plant that will grow when the seed dies.
✤ Thank Jesus for dying to give you new life.

Jesus died on a cross to show
how much he loves us.

He gave his life for us!

Hard things in our lives are called crosses.
Can you accept them with love as Jesus did?

 Do

✤ Finish coloring the jewels to show you have
new life.

A cross is a sign of Jesus' love for us.

When we make the Sign of the Cross,
we show we love God.

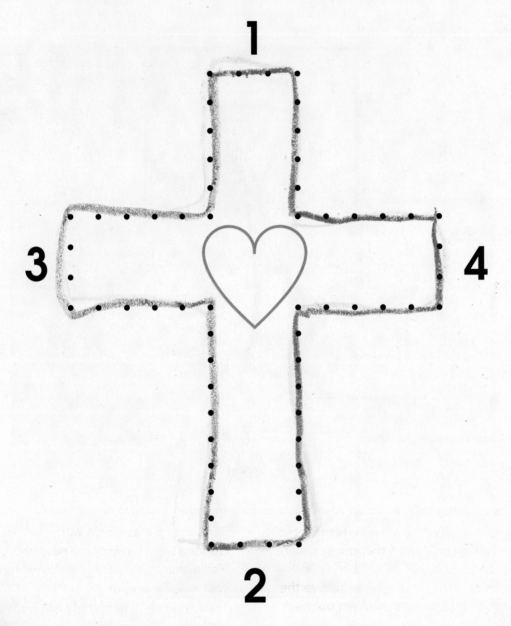

 Do

- Join the dots with a brown crayon to make
  a cross.
- Color the heart red.
- Follow the numbers to help you make the Sign
  of the Cross on yourself.

Butterflies Are Good

20

Sing to the LORD
a new song.

Psalm 149:1

NEW LIFE IN FAMILIES

The Message

Jesus is risen. His victory over sin and death is our triumph as well. We are assured that our yearnings for wholeness and fullness of life will be fulfilled. Although we experience suffering, we believe the power of the Resurrection will transform our pain into new life and glory, and we believe our lives are transformed even now. In this chapter the children are led to wonder and delight in the various forms of new life evident in the spring. They compare the life cycle of a butterfly to Jesus' death and resurrection, and hear that, through baptism, they participate in Jesus' new life and can live his life of love.

Activities

- Read over pages 83–86 with your child.
- Go for a walk and look for new life.
- Visit a church to see the baptismal font where your new life and/or your child's new life began.
- Teach your child to identify some spring flowers. Look for robins. Tell why they are signs of spring.
- Bring new life into your home by buying a small plant or by letting your child pick spring flowers and put them in a vase.
- Read aloud Luke's account of the Resurrection, 24:1–8. Let your child sense your joy in the Easter event and in Jesus' being alive and with us today.

❏ Signature

"My Lord and My God"

A butterfly gives us joy.
It has new life.

On Easter, Jesus rose from
the dead with new life.

We celebrate his new life with great joy.

We sing ALLELUIA!

We can live Jesus' new life.

We can show love
for God and others.

How will you show love?

Signs of Jesus' new life are everywhere in spring.

They tell us to live Jesus' life of love.

Butterflies are signs of Jesus' new life.

Do

✤ Find 8 hidden butterflies and circle them.
✤ Touch each butterfly and whisper "Alleluia" to praise God that Jesus is risen and is with us.

The LORD is my light.

Psalm 27:1

LIGHT IN FAMILIES

The Message

Light conveys life, comfort, and joy. It affects in some way whatever its rays touch. Jesus is the light of the world who seeks to touch us and affect our lives in some way. When we open ourselves to his brightness, the warmth of his love shines through us and touches those close to us. In this chapter the children are led to appreciate light as a gift of God. They hear Jesus call himself the light of the world and learn that the Easter candle is a symbol of Jesus risen. The children are told of the candle they received at baptism to show they share in Jesus' life. They take home "candles" that they made as reminders to let their light shine by being loving to their families.

Activities

- Read over pages 87–90 with your child.
- Visit a church to see the Easter candle. It is a symbol of Jesus, risen and alive.
- Show your child his or her baptismal candle.
- Make or buy a candle as a reminder that Jesus is the light of the world and is present in the midst of your family. Take turns lighting the candle before family prayers. Younger children can blow it out. Decorate it with colored tape, ribbon, or markers.
- Go outside at night and enjoy stargazing.
- Watch a sunrise or sunset.
- Talk about ways you can conserve electricity in order to share God's gift of light with others.

❏ Signature

God knows we need light.
He gives us the gift of the sun.

Jesus is a light for us, too.
He said, "I am the light of the world."

Jesus helps us see how to love God by loving others.

Our hearts are bright with Jesus' love.
Jesus says, "Let your light shine."
He wants his love to shine through us.
We help light up the world with Jesus' love.

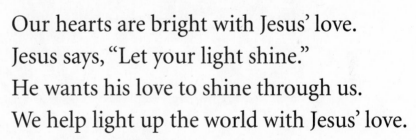

We show love for God and others.

We let the light of Jesus' love shine through us.

 Do

✤ Make the light shine through the darkness.
   Color the rays bright yellow.

✤ How will you bring joy to your family by
   sharing the light of Jesus' love with them?

22 Celebrating Is Good

I will celebrate your love forever, Lord.

Based on Psalm 89:2

CELEBRATING IN FAMILIES

The Message

The Eucharist is at the heart of our Christian lives. We enter into the celebration of Mass most fully when we accept the pains and joys of our lives as our participation in the death and resurrection of Christ. Liturgical formation should be part of children's education. Studies show that children are profoundly affected by early religious experiences. Therefore, parents can begin to teach their children to pray by praying with them. In this chapter the children discover the meaning of gifts and are shown how to thank God for the gifts of his love at the celebration of Mass. The children learn that they are invited, by reason of their baptism, to join in the Sunday Mass celebration.

Activities

- Read over pages 91–94 with your child and let him or her tell you about them. Use the Mass cutouts your child brings home.
- Take your kindergartner to church to celebrate Sunday Mass. Then do something else to make Sunday special.
- Let your child see that singing, praying, and receiving Communion at Mass are important to you.
- Show pictures of family celebrations, such as weddings, baptism, and reunions. Tell how you celebrated these events.
- Encourage your child to listen to the Gospel. Talk about it the week before. Let your child draw a picture of the Gospel message. Post it on the refrigerator.

❑ Signature

Gifts are a sign of love.

We thank people for gifts.

God's gifts are signs of his great love.

We give thanks for God's gifts at Mass.

We celebrate God's love.

Sunday is the Christian day of celebration.

We celebrate with God's family at Mass.

A priest leads the celebration.

We hear God's Word.

We sing and pray and give gifts.

We remember Jesus died and rose with new life.

We thank Jesus for his great love.

God wants us to celebrate his love and
goodness at Sunday Mass.

✤ Draw an altar for the priest celebrating Mass.
✤ Put a candle on each end. Draw a cross in the
   center.
✤ Thank God for inviting you to the Mass.

The Spirit of the LORD fills the whole world.
Based on Wisdom 1:7

THE SPIRIT AT WORK IN FAMILIES

The Message

Jesus promised the gift of his Spirit to enable the Church to fulfill its mission of witnessing to Jesus. His love working through us can transform the world into the kingdom he came to establish. The Greek word *pneuma* can be used for both wind and spirit. In this chapter, after learning about air (wind), an invisible reality that is necessary for life, the children are introduced to the invisible reality of Jesus' Spirit, whose help they need to live as Christians. The Spirit invites us to live Jesus' loving response to God, to love others, and to show responsible stewardship for the earth.

Activities

- Let your child tell you about pages 95–98 as you read them together.
- Open yourself to the inspirations of the Spirit by taking time each day to be alone to think and to pray. When making decisions, pray for guidance.
- Reflect on whether or not your actions indicate you prize persons more than things. Examine how dependent you are on money and things for happiness. Ask whether you use money to develop yourself as a person or to acquire more possessions.
- Encourage your child's growth in wonder by providing opportunities for silence, discovery, sharing, and surprise.
- Engage in healthy, fresh air recreations.

❑ Signature

God gives us the gift of air.

We cannot see air.

We can see what moving air does.

We need air to live.

Jesus gives us the gift of the Holy Spirit.

The Holy Spirit fills us with love.

We cannot see the Holy Spirit.

We can see what love does.

We need the Holy Spirit to love as Jesus did.

Jesus loved Jairus.

Jairus' little girl was very sick.

He asked Jesus for help.

Jesus went with Jairus to his house.

Before they got there, Jairus' daughter died.

Jesus entered the house.

He brought the little girl back to life.

He loved the girl.

Jesus is with us always.

He is with us in his Spirit of Love.

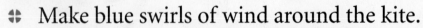

Do

+ Make blue swirls of wind around the kite.
+ Color the kite this way: 1)   ,
  2)   , 3)   . As you color, think
  of loving things you did this week.
+ Touch the heart and ask Jesus' Spirit to fill you
  with love.

Joy Is Good

You fill me with joy.

Based on Psalm 16:11

JOY IN FAMILIES

The Message

Christians have every reason to rejoice. Through his glorious resurrection, Jesus has assured us that we can live in endless joy. He has made it clear, however, that joy does not arise from having selfish desires fulfilled. Rather, it is in sharing the gift of self that we experience the joy Jesus has promised. Family members need reminders of this truth because they sometimes cause conflict by seeking their own interests. In this chapter the children learn that Jesus risen is the source of Christian joy and that they are called to be joy-bringers. They are encouraged to go beyond self-centeredness, to reach out to others in self-sacrificing love, and to bring joy to those whom they meet.

Activities

- Read pages 99–102 with your child and invite him or her to tell you about them.
- Include fun activities in your family life. Watch a good TV comedy and enjoy laughing together.
- Tell your child that seeing him or her happy gives you joy and pleases Jesus. Being happy is one way of spreading Jesus' joy.
- Do something this week as a family to bring joy to someone outside the immediate family.
- Help your child realize that disappointments and hardships are part of everyone's life and cannot take away our deep inner joy unless we let them.
- At the evening meals this week, let the family members tell how other members bring them joy.

❑ Signature

Jesus brought joy to the world.

He wants us to share his joy.

Loving and helping others brings
them joy.

It brings us joy, too.

Look at the pictures on pages 100 and 101.

Who is giving joy to others?

Who needs joy? How would you bring joy to them?

Christians bring joy to others.

We show that we  love God.

✤ Draw a line from each joy balloon to a person who is receiving joy.

✤ Color the balloons.

✤ Touch each balloon and ask God to help you bring joy to others.

You show me the path to life.

Based on Psalm 16:11

LIFE AND DEATH IN FAMILIES

The Message

Death is a mystery. The greatest gift God has given is the precious gift of life, yet it is only in dying that we are born to eternal life. Life reaches fullness in heaven. God alone can satisfy the desires of the human person. In union with the blessed in heaven, including our loved ones, we will experience perfect joy. In this chapter the children recall that new life comes through death. They are led to realize that they, too, will die one day. After becoming aware of the nobler human joys of beauty and love, the children learn that the greatest joy of heaven will be experiencing God's overwhelming love. They will also enjoy the company of the blessed.

Activities

- Read over pages 103–106 with your child and encourage him or her to tell you about them.
- Help your child to be aware of how God fills the world with life, and teach your child to show reverence for life in all its forms.
- Visit grandparents, so your child learns respect for the elderly and learns that aging is part of life.
- Express joy at the birth of babies among relatives and friends.
- When someone dies, explain that you grieve because you miss the loved one, but you know the person has a new life with God.
- Although your child cannot understand death, do not try to hide this reality of life from him or her. Pray for those who have died.

❏ Signature

Jesus gave us a life that will never end.

We have this life now.

We will have it forever in heaven.

Jesus lives in heaven with the Father and the Holy Spirit.

He lives in us, too.

One day Jesus will come in glory.

He will gather us together in his kingdom.

There will be no more sadness or tears.

We will be together with God and Mary, the saints, and all our loved ones.

In heaven we will be happy forever because

WE  love GOD.

Jesus said his kingdom is like a great treasure.

 Do

❖ With a pencil follow the path that leads to the treasure.

❖ Thank God for giving you his life so that you can live forever.

❖ Ask Jesus to help you choose to act in loving ways that lead to the kingdom.

Easter Flowers

The Voortmann family celebrates the new life of spring and Easter with a delightful custom. At the end of September they plant crocus bulbs and hope the flowers will bloom at Easter time. They set the bulbs in holes a few inches deep that have been dug to form a cross, an egg, a banner, or words such as *Alleluia, New Life,* or *He is risen.* They then hold a prayer celebration by sprinkling the bulbs in the ground with holy water and reading Jesus' words in John 12:24 from the Bible:

> Amen, amen, I say to you, unless a grain of wheat falls to the ground and dies, it remains just a grain of wheat; but if it dies, it produces much fruit.

In the spring the flowers come up in the shape they were planted and declare an Easter message to everyone who sees them. They are a sign of the new life of Christ that we will share forever.

Your family might wish to do this during the coming year, or you might simply place colorful Easter eggs on the ground in the spring to form an Easter symbol to celebrate new life.

Our Church

Take your child to church with you for a visit or for Mass. Point out features of the church, such as the altar, the tabernacle, the crucifix, and a stained-glass window. When you return home, have your child draw in this frame something he or she saw in church.

The Cross

The cross is a sign of Jesus' love for us. Help your child find and circle the cross on the steeple and the nine crosses hidden in this picture.

New Life

Jesus brought us new life by dying on the cross and rising from the dead. Search through magazines and newspapers for pictures of new life, such as a bud, a chick, a baby, or a kitten. Help your child cut out the pictures and paste them in the cross below, or have your child draw pictures of new life.

SUPPLEMENT

Special People and Special Days

Mary Is Good

Mary is the mother of Jesus.

She is our heavenly mother.

We celebrate her birthday on September 8.

 Do

- Color Mary's cake to make it look like the kind you like best.
- Decorate the cake with pretty flowers. Put more candles on it.
- Greet Mary by saying "Hail Mary." Then wish her a happy birthday.

A picture story

Do

 Ask the Little Flower of Jesus to help you love God.

Angel sent by God to guide me,

be my light and walk beside me.

Be my guardian and protect me.

On the paths of life direct me.

Amen.

Do

✤ Trace around the child praying.

✤ Say a prayer to your guardian angel.

St. Francis loved everything
God made.

He called these things
his brothers and sisters.

- Trace around the animals, flowers, and sun and color them.
- Touch each one and thank God for it.
- Call it your brother or sister as Francis did. Say, "Thank you, God, for Brother Rabbit."

St. Nicholas was a kind bishop.

He surprised people with acts of love.

He helped the poor.

Do

❖ Put a bishop's hat on St. Nicholas. Color it yellow.

❖ Put a bag of gold coins in his hand.

The wise men went to see Jesus.

They gave him three gifts.

I will give him the gift of my love.

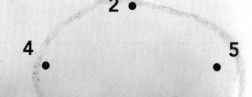

♦ Connect the dots to make the star.
♦ Color the gifts. Tell Jesus that you love him as you color them.
♦ Make smoke come from the middle wise man's incense.

Mary and Joseph took Jesus to the Temple.

Simeon offered Jesus to God our Father.

He called Jesus the light of the world.

Light

Do

- Trace over the letters and color them.
- Touch the word **light** and thank God for sending Jesus as the light of the world.

Mary visited Bernadette long ago.

Mary asked for prayers and sacrifices.

We do what Mary asked.

Do

✤ Color the rays yellow.
✤ Color the water blue.
✤ Color the roses yellow.

Lent Is Good

In spring we plant seeds.
We help them grow.
Lent is like springtime.
It is a time for us to grow.
We grow as God's children.

A seed grows into a plant.
Leaves and buds grow on it.
During Lent, we grow in
God's love.
We pray and do good deeds.

LENT IN FAMILIES

Activities

- Let your child tell about pages 116 and 117.
- On the evening of Ash Wednesday, plant some seeds in a flowerpot and set the pot in a sunny place. Decide on a motto, such as "Love Grows," "To Love Is to Grow," or "Lent Is a Time of Loving." Print it on a piece of paper. Prick the paper through with a toothpick and stake it into the flowerpot. Then watch and pray that love will grow.
- Decide on a Lenten sacrifice that you could do together as a family. Use your kitchen calendar to note your daily successes or failures in keeping your resolutions.
- Participate in Operation Rice Bowl if possible.

- Pray together each night. Look at the crucifix and share some short prayers, such as "O Jesus, how much you have loved us! Help us to love you, too."
- During every week of Lent do something special and kind for a person or family—someone who is poor, sick, or lonely. Go out of your way to do it.
- Together as a family, do something kind for each other every day.
- Each night thank God for specific graces of the day.
- Think of ways in which your family can show a change of heart toward other people.

❏ Signature

By Easter the plant has many flowers.

By Easter our hearts should be full of love.

Do

✤ Color all the leaves.

✤ Each time you say a prayer or do a good deed during Lent, color one heart petal on the plant.

117

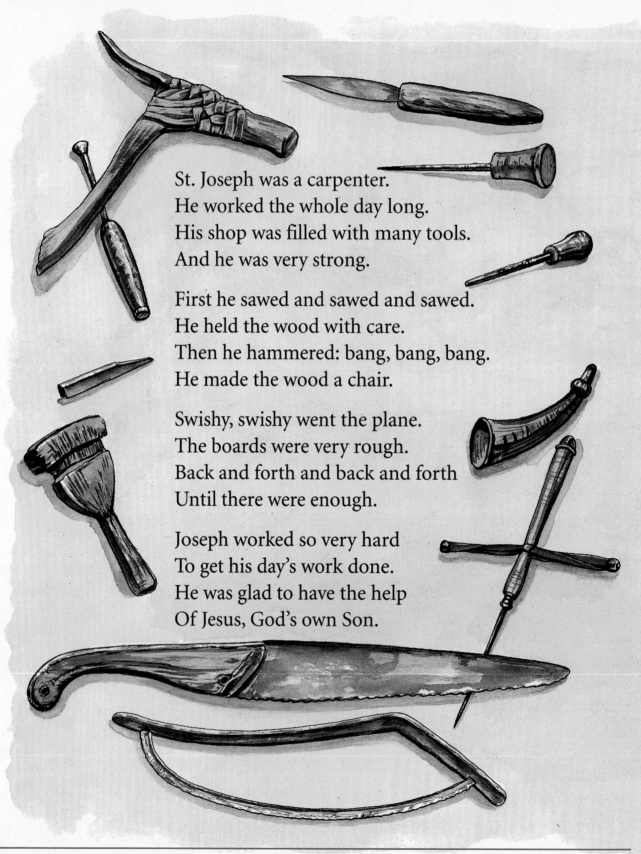

St. Joseph was a carpenter.
He worked the whole day long.
His shop was filled with many tools.
And he was very strong.

First he sawed and sawed and sawed.
He held the wood with care.
Then he hammered: bang, bang, bang.
He made the wood a chair.

Swishy, swishy went the plane.
The boards were very rough.
Back and forth and back and forth
Until there were enough.

Joseph worked so very hard
To get his day's work done.
He was glad to have the help
Of Jesus, God's own Son.

Joseph took care of Jesus and Mary.
Joseph was a good man.
Jesus helped Joseph.

St. Julie was a sister.

She taught children to love God.

Sisters have a special love for God.

They are his special helpers.

This sister is teaching the children to love God.

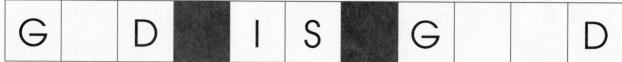

| G | D | | I | S | | G | | D |

✣ Print **O** in the empty blocks.

✣ Then read what Julie taught.

Chapter 1

Chapter 12 ⇨

JESUS

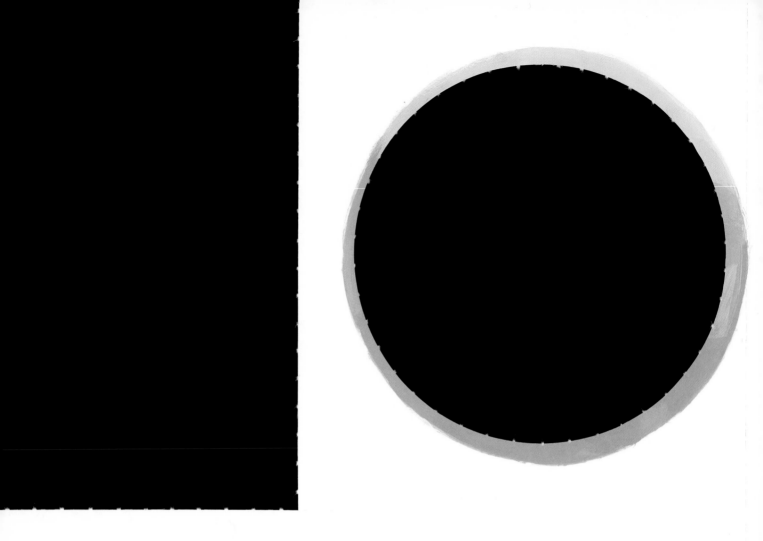

Chapter 2

Father in heaven,
our hearts desire
    the warmth of your love;
our minds are searching
    for the light of your Word.

Increase our longing for Jesus
and help us grow in love
that we may rejoice
    in his presence
and welcome his light in our lives.
We pray in the name of Jesus the Lord.
                    Amen.

Amen

Our Father

Chapter 11

Chapter 12 ⇩

Our Father, who art in heaven,
hallowed be thy name;
thy kingdom come;
thy will be done on earth
as it is in heaven.

Give us this day our daily bread;
and forgive us our trespasses
as we forgive those
who trespass against us;
and lead us not into temptation,
but deliver us from evil.
Amen.

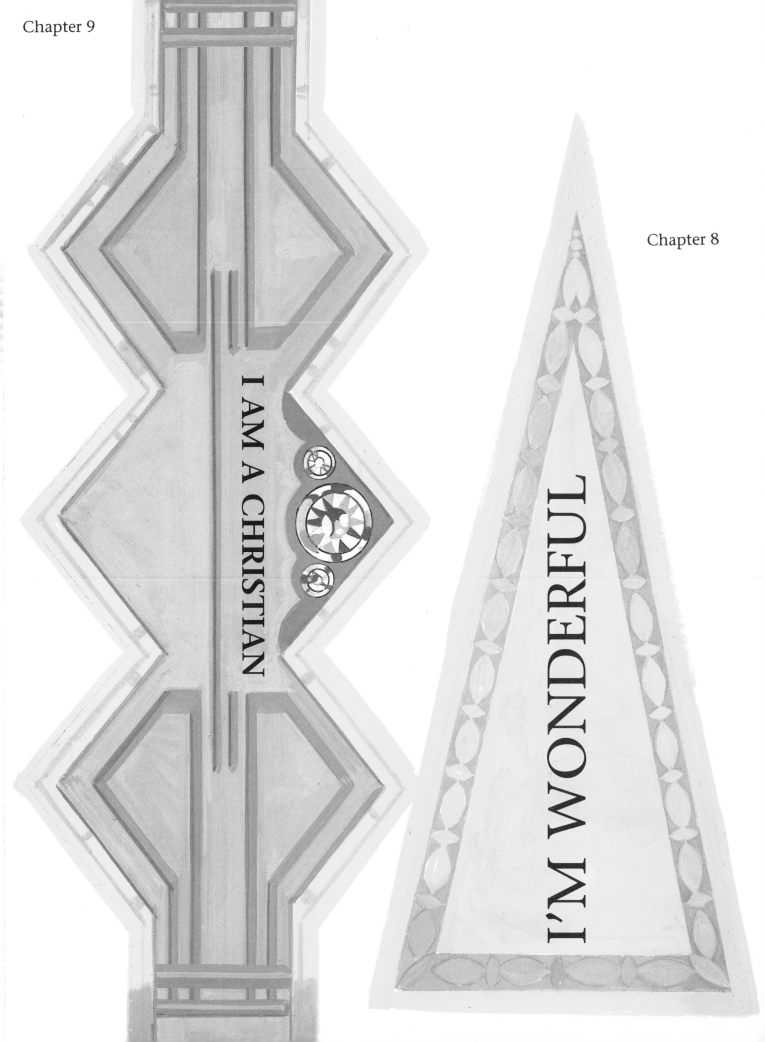

Chapter 9

I AM A CHRISTIAN

Chapter 8

I'M WONDERFUL

Bless us, O Lord,
and these your gifts
which we are about to receive
from your bounty,
through Christ our Lord.
Amen.

Supplement, Chapter 7

Chapter 10

Chapter 21

YES

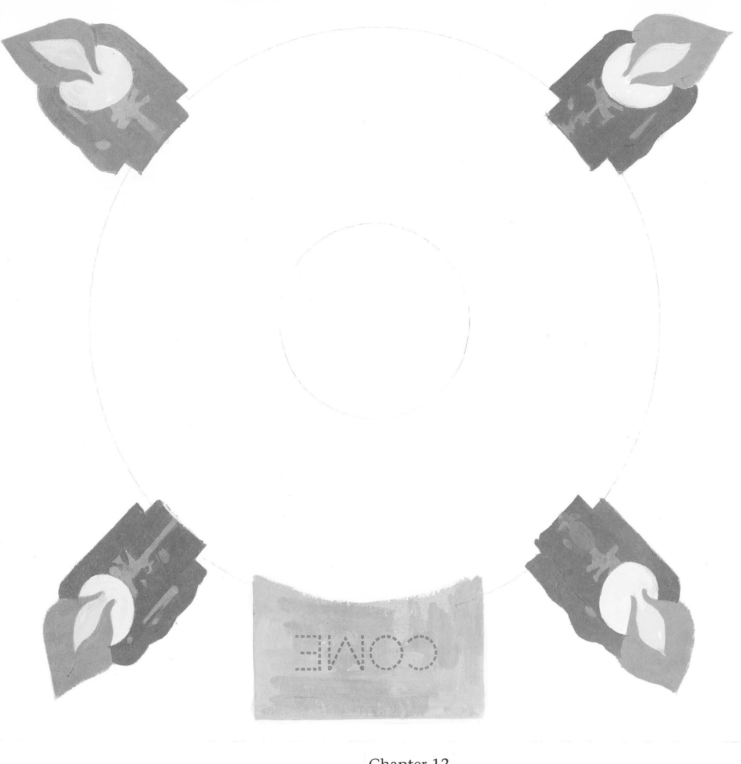

Chapter 12

glue to part b

Chapter 16

Jesus

Chapter 14

Chapter 19

ALLELUIA

Chapter 20

ALLELUIA

Jesus loves us.

Jesus
is
risen!

ALLELUIA

Jesus
is
risen!

ALLELUIA

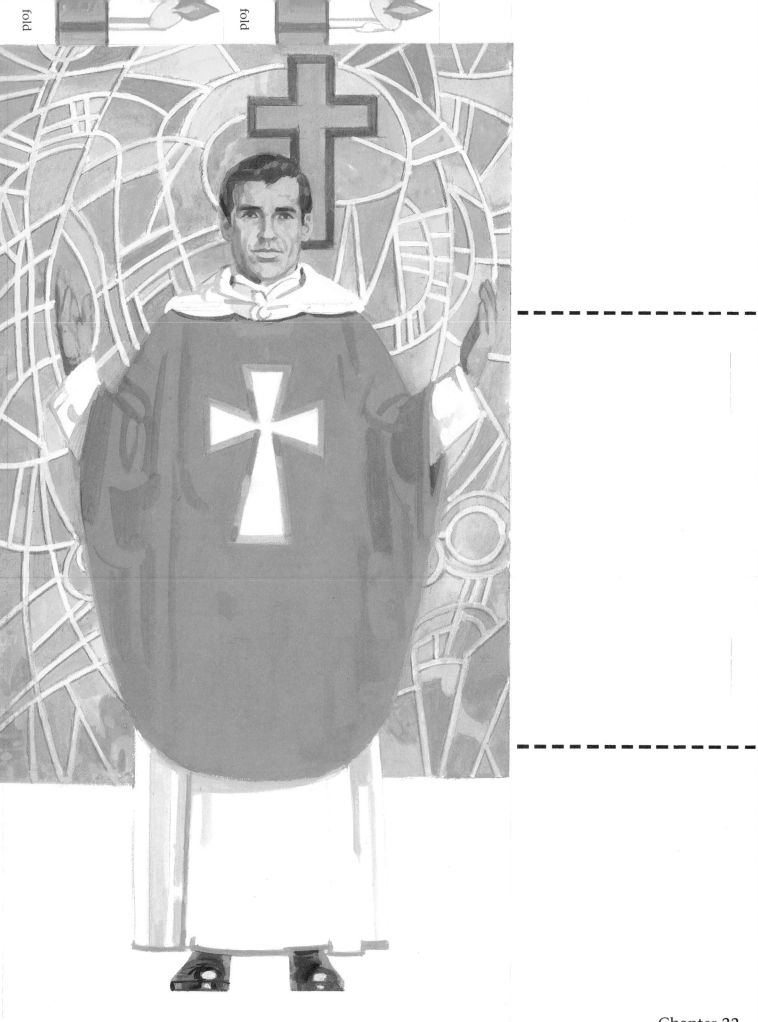